TIGER MOTHS TO TYPHOONS

by

PETER WATSON
F/Lt RAFVR

THE STORY OF A WORLD WAR TWO FIGHTER PILOT

EDITED BY ANDY & SUE PARLOUR

TEN BELLS PUBLISHING LTD

Published 2000 by Ten Bells Publishing Ltd
Registered Office
Springbank House
20, Spring Road
St. Osyth
Essex CO16 8RP

Copyright 2000 Ten Bells Publishing Ltd

ISBN No 0 9531269 35 (pbk)

Introduction and Acknowledgements

My name is Peter Watson, and I am an ex-World War II fighter-pilot.

It has been suggested to me that, as there aren't many of us left, I should record my experiences for, shall we say, posterity. Partly that the younger generation, who have now become interested in this sort of thing, may read it, and partly, since it all happened about 55 to 60 years ago, it is now a subject of modern history.

So, I am going to tell my story as best I can, and hope it interests you.

But firstly, I would like to take the time to thank some friends without whose encouragement my story might never have seen the light of day.

To Roy Willard, my 'secretary', for all his kindness, patience and time spent helping me. It would have been a mammoth task without his support.

To Chris Parker for his computer knowledge and know-how.

To Denis Somerville Baddeley for his aviation expertise.

Special thanks to Andy and Sue Parlour for putting my story together, editing it and having the determination and confidence to go ahead and publish it.

To all of them my heartfelt thanks

Peter Watson
Bexhill-on-Sea
2000

Dedication

"I am dedicating this story to the average sort of pilot, such as I was myself, and there must have been thousands of us, but not only pilots, all aircrew too.

Some of us survived - we were <u>destined</u> to survive. Many of us didn't.

But, as I say, this story is really dedicated to the average pilot and aircrew, to my friends who were either killed or taken prisoner, of which these must have been about 80%. We must not forget them.

At the same time, I can't let this story go without expressing my admiration for the ground crews that kept us going. We had a relationship that was a <u>team</u> relationship. We were friends rather than on officer-and-airman terms, and we knew that we relied on them to keep us in the air, which they made a marvellous job of. My gratitude goes out to them."

Peter Watson
Bexhill-on-Sea
2000

Foreword

"I would like to say that you will have to forgive me if I am not entirely accurate about my facts because we are talking about something that happened between 55 and 60 years ago, and I'm doing this entirely from memory.

In telling this story, I have tried to make it interesting for the reader by not dwelling on the morbid parts of it but by making it partly humorous. There were sad parts in it, whereby the saddest parts were when I saw my best friends, fellow pilots, come down. Shot down either in a ball of flames or perhaps into the sea. I even saw a couple of them crash-land on the airstrip and they were burnt alive."

Peter Watson
Bexhill-on-Sea
2000

CHAPTER ONE

In 1939, when the war-clouds were gathering, I was a boarder at Cranbrook Public School. Although I scraped through the normal Matric. exams, my main interests were the Officers' Training Corps and rifle-range shooting, but my main ambition was to fly.

When I left school the war was well on its way. The evacuation of the British Expeditionary Force from Dunkirk was taking place at the end of May 1940 and we seemed to be getting the worst of it.

Now at 17, although I was of small stature, but with my father's consent, I went to a recruitment centre where I volunteered for Air-Crew.

I passed the necessary medicals and interviews but was put on what was called 'Deferred Service'. For some reason or other we were not permitted to fly until we were 17 and a third, but this suited me as I was able to join the Home Guard while the Battle of Britain was raging overhead.

We had great fun in the Home Guard, with bayonets attached to the end of broomsticks, .303 rifles and molotov cocktails with which to repel the supposedly heavily-armed German invaders if they ever got up as far as Surrey. To add to the excitement, dog-fights were daily occurrences overhead and I watched the Spitfires and Hurricanes operating with pride and envy.

I had my calling-up papers at the same time as a Reigate friend of mine, Archie Mortimer, who was the same age as myself. He was very keen, bright-eyed and robust, which was to turn out to my advantage. We had to meet at Victoria Station to take a train to Torquay where there was a Reception Centre. This seemed like going to a holiday-camp - but it was not. Here we began our basics. My friend Archie helped me in making up the bed, kit inspections, button and boot-polishing, etc., at which I was no good.

Initial Training Wing was our next stop where we had to endure rigorous physical training, drill, and elementary Ground Lectures. I was fairly hopeless at this and I think I only got through because they were getting desperate for pilots.

For instance, I was no good at Morse. So when the exam came - we had to do this by Aldis-lamp with the Instructor at the other end of the green - and my name was called, I persuaded another friend of mine, Philips, to take my place. He did so reluctantly, and I got lOO%! Later on Philips' own test came, but by now he was shattered, and failed. He was not very pleased about this as it meant he had to take the test again, which he did, and only passed with 90%!

Rather to everyone's surprise, I was passed out as average pilot-material from Initial Training Wing and, after some leave, I was posted to an Elementary Flying Training School at Brough, near Hull, in Yorkshire. Here the object of the operation was for us to learn to fly on TIGER MOTHS.

On the ground we were put in the care of a Flight-Sergeant Small. He was a nice old chap of about 30 who seemed rather overwhelmed by having to control a course of twenty lively and healthy schoolboys, which virtually we were

His worst times were when we came back to the billet after the local pub closed at night. This was often the cue for boisterous play, with beds being overturned, trousers pulled off and thrown out of windows, and suchlike. I have to admit that I usually instigated these battles.

It then became the lot of Pilot Officer Mason to be my Flying Instructor. He was also a nice chap, an ex-schoolmaster who took things rather seriously. He took me up 'dual' in the Tiger Moth and put me through the hoops, teaching me takeoffs and landings, or 'circus and bumps' as we used to call them, to spins, stalls and aerobatics. He seemed rather dubious about my progress as it was probably somewhat rather erratic depending on the amount of sherbet I'd consumed the previous night.

Poor Pilot Officer Mason literally reached the end of his tether when he had to take me on a cross country navigation test over the wilds of Yorkshire with myself as pilot, for, of course, I got hopelessly lost.

With the cloud-base down to about 500 feet and the fuel guage indicating not much above zero, he cried out over the intercom, rather hysterically I thought, for me to look for a field in which to make a forced landing. I spotted a suitable place adjacent to a village and hopefully, I thought, the village pub as well. We approached just over the tree-tops and under the telegraph wires and made rather a bumpy landing. We tethered the Tiger down with the help of some bewildered locals, all the while being watched by a couple of interested cows. Then we went to the pub, where Pilot Officer Mason telephoned a Mayday to the base while I smartly sank a beer and a whisky chaser.

After a couple of hours of this, the cavalry arrived in the form of a truck containing some fuel and a rather irate Chief Flying Instructor, who had to fly the Tiger back to base while Pilot Officer Mason and I were driven back by truck in some disgrace.

However, as the Instructor was captain, I was not held responsible for this misdemeanour but poor Pilot Officer Mason got a bit of a rocket.

The next morning I went up for some more 'dual' instruction with my rather shattered Instructor. When we landed, he indicated that I should stay in the cockpit and keep the engine running. Then he got out, slapped me on the shoulder and shouted:

"You're going solo, lad!" Then added, "You'll make it all right." Being rather given to the dramatic, he then stood back, saluted, and waved me out. Unfortunately, neither of us had noticed some barbed-wire fencing in my path. I taxied right into it, causing only some superficial damage to the airframe, but nevertheless making it impossible for me to take off.

That afternoon I was called up before the Chief Flying Instructor (CFI), a Squadron Leader Steel. He was a fabulous person. Ex-operational and a Distinguished Flying Cross (DFC) holder complete with a Ronald Coleman moustache and an untidy scarf. He told me I was to have one last chance, a C.F.I.'s test. This was, more often than not, the 'out' signal. Once in the Tiger, Squadron Leader Steel called out over the intercom that she was all mine and that I was to do just as he instructed. First to climb to 5,000 feet. This I did. Then, without warning, he cut the engine switches. The engine went dead.

"Get out of that," he yelled - and laughed.

I instinctively pushed the stick forward to get the aircraft into a nose-dive situation. The only way to restart the engine was to make a steep dive so as to rotate the propellor to suitable revs, giving it some throttle at the same time, but not too much so as not to flood the carburettor. Rather like bump-starting a car, you know.

Down to about 2,500 feet I shouted over the intercom, "Right, Sir, switches on, please?"

Squadron Leader Steel complied. The engine restarted beauti-
fully and I pulled out at about 1,000 feet, but the Chief Flying
Instructor had by no means finished with me yet.

He instructed me to climb back up to 5,000 feet. He then told
me to do a loop, a roll, and then a stall into a spin and get
out of it. This I did. And although I say it myself, the performance was perfect. I landed the Tiger Moth as gently as a
butterfly on a daisy and then taxied back to Dispersal very
carefully.

Later on I was summoned to the C.F.I.'s office. I stood before
him awaiting the verdict. When our eyes met, I knew we had
an affinity.

"You've passed your flying test," he began."However, Flight-
Sergeant Small reports that you are unruly on the ground,
start fights, and generally misbehave."

I held his gaze while he continued, "Why must you be so
aggressive - particularly as with your size you usually get the
worst of it?"

Squadron Leader Steel went on: "I see you've applied to
become a fighter-pilot - that's probably why you're so aggressive."

He fixed me with his eye. "But I must warn you that if you do
get through, which is very doubtful, you won't survive a day
on a fighter squadron. So," he said, "you'd better mend your
ways." He paused. "But I am recommending you to go on for
further training, but behave yourself."

I said, "Thank you very much, Sir." And I'm quite sure, as he
dismissed me, that he winked at me. Anyway, I left that inter-
view feeling quite happy.

I was then posted to Ansty, which was an aerodrome just outside Coventry, for a night-flying course, which turned out to
be more hair-raising than anything I'd ever done before - or
after, I think.

It was deep winter, snow was on the ground, the conditions
were icy and we were flying open-cockpit Tiger Moths with
hardly any instruments at all. We were flying just outside
Coventry, which was surrounded by barrage-balloons, and,
because Coventry had been heavily blitzed, the anti-aircraft
gunners were a bit trigger-happy. However, I survived and
managed to fly solo in the black of night, not knowing where
I was or what I was doing, and each time I seemed to get the
aeroplane down safely again.

There were one or two consolations about the night-flying course. One was that we used to have a 'night-flying breakfast' about five o'clock in the morning, which consisted of eggs and bacon and coffee. Then we had the most beautiful sleep. We had very comfortable double-roomed billets which were centrally-heated. I shared mine with 'Tosh' Kitchen. (I don't quite know why we called him Tosh) He was a nice sort of chap, but just a little eccentric, shall we say.

What we used to do, even if we hadn't been night-flying, was to hang a little notice outside the door saying: DO NOT DISTURB - NIGHT-FLYING. This meant that we could sort of hibernate in peace during the ghastly weather, and we would take it in turns to stagger over to the canteen to fetch either some food or cups of tea. All quite civilised really.

The only thing was that, as I soon discovered, Tosh had rather a strange habit. In the middle of the night, he would get out of bed and, instead of going to the toilet - he insisted this happened in his sleep - he would urinate into a flying-boot, but he never used to urinate in his own, always mine. I got a bit fed up with this in the end, so, before he went to sleep every night, I used to make sure that he went to use the toilet. I took the opportunity, while he was out of the room, to hide my boots - usually under my bed. However, that was his only bad habit and apart from that he was an awfully nice chap.

Anyway, as I say, we did manage to survive this particular course, despite the precarious situations we often found ourselves in, and I successfully passed the course and again went on leave.

CHAPTER TWO

At the end of this leave I received instructions and the necessary railway warrant to report to another Reception Centre called Heaton Park, just outside Manchester. It had, I believe, been a zoo at some time. It was now generally known to be a centre where you got kitted-out for going overseas.

Although we weren't supposed to know our destination overseas, we did. We knew that this was going to be Canada, and that we would in fact be sailing from Greenock, near Glasgow, in Scotland. So in due course we were all transported up to Scotland, bound ultimately for Halifax, Nova Scotia.

We set sail and joined a convoy, as was usual then when crossing the Atlantic. The journey proved to be very tedious because it took us ten days to get to Halifax since we constantly had to zig-zag in order to avoid being easy meat for the German U-boats. Fortunately, they didn't find us.

On board this troopship the conditions were ghastly - we were about three-deep in the hold. It was, I believe, a French ship called the 'Normandie'. Although, as I say, it was a bit squalid, we did get to Halifax safely and from there we were herded on to trains and we crossed Canada in quite a civilised sort of way.

Another Reception Centre and then I was dispersed to a place called Swiftcurrent, in Saskatchewan. By this time my friend and guardian, Archie Mortimer, had again joined me. Swiftcurrent was a delightful little place on Swiftcurrent Creek, west of Regina and just north-east of the Cypress Hills. The United States began just south of here.

I mainly remember Swiftcurrent because of the fact that all the streetlights were on and you could have the most enormous steaks and things - marvellous food. This after coming from England where there was a blackout and very little food. I also seem to remember that half of the inhabitants were these sort of Red Indian chaps off the Reservation who used to wear bowler hats and pigtails - but they were quite nice with it really.

On arrival we were taken out to the aerodrome itself where we learnt that we were to be introduced to the North American Harvard, a trainer. I found the Harvard a very nice aeroplane to fly. It was very noisy but quite manoeuverable, a sort of cut between a Tiger Moth and a fighter aeroplane like a Hurricane or a Spitfire, as I was to find out later.

Although I say I found it quite pleasant to fly, I'm afraid my Instructor didn't entirely agree as he found my manoeuvres somewhat erratic. But, nevertheless, I pressed on and towards the end of the course, when again my Instructor wasn't very happy with me, I had to go through the ordeal of another Chief Flying Instructor's test.

Well, I had this test with a C.F.I. who was again, as was my luck, a splendid chap with whom I seemed to have an affinity. Again he put me through the hoop - I did all sorts of things like aerobatics, precautionary landings, forced landings, and so on and so forth, and he couldn't fault me. So when we came down, I followed him into the crew room where I overheard him talking to my Instructor. I think he was giving him a bit of a rocket for criticising my flying.

Anyway, the result of it was that, subject to my passing the 'ground' exams - we were having lectures about this side of it all the time - I would get my wings.

But, as in the past, I was having trouble with my 'ground' exams.

Again, I had a little bit of luck. There was another cadet on our training course whose name was Pringle. He had this habit of crashing the aeroplanes - particularly on coming in to land. This he did to such an extent that we in fact called him 'Pranger' Pringle. The poor fellow was grounded, you know, because they just couldn't afford all these Harvards being bent and so on.

I turned his disadvantage into my advantage. Pringle, you see, had been put in the Orderly room where it just so happened they typed out all the exam-papers for the 'ground' exams. Fortunately, I was able to get from 'Pranger' a full copy of the tests that we were going to receive the next day. During that night we burned the midnight oil and, with the aid of a couple of text-books, got the answers all ready.

Of course, we sailed through the 'ground' exams with a high percentage mark. So that was it.

We were duly presented to some Air Marshal or other who congratulated us on our efficiency and pinned wings on our chests. Archie Mortimer actually went through the exam with genuine flying colours because of his proficiency, and he came out a Pilot Officer. I thought myself very lucky to come out a

Sergeant Pilot. In any case, we were all now very happy with life. We were granted a week or so leave at Swiftcurrent, whereby we whooped it up somewhat in the town. All the girls seemed to quite like us, particularly as we had the 'wings' up and all that sort of thing.

We apparently, I remember, had quite a bit of money and, without going into too much detail, we did have a very good couple of weeks leave before being shipped back to the United Kingdom - again under the most appalling conditions. But we were so anxious to get back home, despite the hospitality of the Canadians, that we readily put up with the conditions, eventually arriving back at that same place we had originally embarked from, Greenock, in Scotland. Again we were sent on leave.

CHAPTER THREE

I spent this leave with my parents and sister at Redhill in Surrey. Looking back, I can't help thinking how marvellous they were to me. Obviously they made quite a fuss of me. It must have been dreadful for them because they were having a much worse time than I was. And, of course, they realised that the chances of my getting killed were increasing all the time. They must have been really in a terrible state of anxiety but they didn't show it.

As usual, while on leave I got my next marching-orders, which this time were for me to report to an Advanced Flying Training School up near Peterborough where we would have to learn to fly MASTERS. This was to adjust us to flying in the United Kingdom rather than the more comfortable conditions that we had enjoyed over in Canada.

From Peterborough we were transferred straight on to an Operational Training Unit which was up near Alnwick in Northumberland. Here we were going to learn to fly HURRI-CANES.

It was about this time that I received the awful news that poor Archie Mortimer, my longtime friend, who had been so proficient that he'd been appointed an Instructor in Canada on Harvards, had had a collision in a formation with a pupil and had been killed. Whereas I was still going strong.

When we did gather at this School near Alnwick, we were, I well remember, in awe of the aeroplane that we had got to fly - the Hurricane. Because if you think about it, you see, you can't have any 'dual' instruction on an aeroplane like that. The Instructor can only pop you in the cockpit, tell you what to do, how the aeroplane may be expected to react to the way you handle it, and then off you go and hope for the best!

Well, this seemed to work with me because I really got on well with the Hurricane. I found it a marvellous aeroplane to fly and I seemed to be able to handle it quite well. Once more through all the usual stages of 'circus and bumps' and then on to aerobatics and so on to close-formation flying.

At Alnwick I'd met up with another old friend, Howell Head. He was a great chap, but we were sort of 'friendly enemies' if you can imagine. If ever we saw each other in the sky we used to have the most grisly dog-fights you could ever envisage. It really is a wonder that we didn't kill each other. This was sort of accepted - though it wasn't really approved - but it was accepted that we did this sort of thing.

One night, when we'd had quite a few drinks in the mess, he made a challenge to me that we should have a dog-fight with a ceiling of 500 feet. In other words, everything had to happen in the low-flying area below 500 feet, which is a little bit grisly.

After a few more drinks we all went to bed and I forgot all about it. But he hadn't. In the dim dawn of next morning, Howell woke me up.

"Come on! Wake up, 'Trigger'."

I must explain that I was called 'Trigger' at this stage because I had got a bit of a name for having a good eye and being a good shot on the shooting-ranges.

I said: "Oh, go away, Howell, for gawd's sake."

But he absolutely insisted that we'd got to carry out this vendetta.

We stumbled out into the murky dawn, took a Hurricane each, and climbed aboard. By the way, the best thing if you've got a hangover is, when you get into your aeroplane, to put your oxygen mask on, turn the gas up as if you're flying at about 30,000 feet or so, so you're getting full oxygen, and stick your head out of the cockpit so that you get the slipstream from the propellor. This soon clears your head, which is just as well.

Well, we took off in formation and split. Then we turned and approached each other head-on below our 500 feet deadline, in the low-flying area. It was a matter of who would break first.

Hopefully, one would break before the other, but on this occasion we both sort of, not literally, but sort of stuck to our guns, and we were very, very close to each other when we both split. (You split to starboard, by the way; each of you split to starboard.) Then we diced around, each trying to get on the other's tail, but neither of us succeeded so we called it an honourable draw and returned to base.

This sort of thing went on for as long as we were training together but, in all that time, it was only towards the end of the training course that I had one minor prang, and that was due to a tyre that burst on landing. I'm afraid I pranged the Hurricane and got a little bit of a rocket from the Chief Flying Instructor.

The Chief Flying Instructor was a pretty hard man. To pass out you had to go through a test with him. His aeroplane was painted completely black, so naturally he was known to us as 'the black bastard'.

Here again you would take off with him in formation and then split and a dog-fight would ensue. If you were absolutely hopeless and he would obviously be able to shoot you down, then you would fail the course. If, however, you put up a reasonable show, then you would be passed out.

Well, I whizzed about the sky with him trying to get on my tail but I managed to take the necessary evasive action and finally found a bit of cloud and hid up in it so that he couldn't catch me. Eventually we landed and I'd successfully got through yet another course.

Before being unleashed on an unsuspecting European Theatre of War as an operational pilot, I had to go before the Flight Commander at R.A.F. Millfield, which is the aerodrome at the Operational Training Unit, in order to have a general assessment. The Flight Commander glared at me and informed me that, although my flying ability seemed to be average, my behaviour on the ground had not been entirely up to standard as I had two adverse reports.

These reports I will explain.

There did exist a sort of running feud between the Nissen hut next door to us, which contained six Sergeant Pilots, and the six of us in our hut, also Sergeant Pilots. To put it another way, a certain amount of a sort of friendly animosity and competition pertained, and this became a source of scenes and squabbles.

I decided one night in the mess, together with my five chaps from our Nissen hut, on a scheme.

We had bicycles on this aerodrome to get from A to B, for instance to Dispersal and back to our billets or wherever. Now this scheme was that when the mess closed, I gathered my chaps and got them to follow me fairly smartish down to our Nissen hut. This we did. It was a very dark night. We belted down to the entrance to the billets which, in fact, was a fairly narrow gap. Under my instructions, we all laid our bicycles down in the middle of the path and waited for our 'prey' to arrive. Which they soon did - and at high speed. When they got to the obstructed entrance they were unable to stop and the six of them crashed heavily into my trap, just as I'd intended.

Immediately we leapt on them and, although this might have been grossly unfair, the tactics had worked. As they were already half-stunned from coming off their bikes, it didn't take much from us to totally put them to flight, although we didn't do them any serious damage, of course. They were so much in awe of this terrorism that they thereafter locked themselves firmly in their Nissen hut, for fear of further action from us.

This escapade had come to the attention of the Flight Sergeant Disciplinarian who had made a report of it and had given me a good telling off about it as I was the instigator.

So, the Commander knew I'd had a reprimand for that, and he also reminded me of another instance where I'd had a fight with one Sergeant Slack.

Sergeant Slack had alleged I'd beaten him up in the cycle-shed outside the Sergeants' Mess. He claimed that he'd said that I didn't like him and he didn't like me, and that I had said, "Well, nobody likes Sergeant Slack!" Further, that one night he had come up to me in the mess and accused me of letting his bicycle tyres down out in the shed, and that I had said, "Well, I didn't let your damn tyres down, but if I'd thought about it I would have done."

This had prompted Sergeant Slack to say, "Well, perhaps we'd better go out there and sort it out."

In the meantime, a more recently-made friend of mine, a Welshman named 'Taffy' Powell, another Sergeant Pilot, and a fairly tough fellow, had been listening in on this conversation between Sergeant Slack and myself while he was downing a pint. 'Taffy' could down a pint very smartly, by the way. He also, which was rather fortunate for me, was, I think, an amateur boxer in Wales before he'd come into the R.A.F. and was an amateur champion of some sort.

Anyway, I went out to this bicycle shed with the said Sergeant Slack where it was fairly murky and dark and squared up to him. He got hold of me by the lapels and I thought, "Oh, Lord! This is it.", because he was bigger than I was.

He was about to hit me when he suddenly disappeared and I thought, "Where's he gone?"

Well, Slack had gone whizzing back, on his back, into the cycle-shed and he was suddenly lying there with all the bicycle-wheels and pedals turning round about him. He was out like a light, a goner.

What had happened was that my friend, 'Taffy' Powell, realising the situation, that I might well come to some harm on this occasion, had followed us out to the shed, come up behind us in the semi-darkness and whopped Slack over my shoulder in a most professional manner, very effectively knocking him out.

I turned round and seeing 'Taffy' said, "Oh, thanks. Thanks very much, Taffy. I think I probably owe you a drink."

"Yes, I think you do," replied 'Taffy'.

Whereupon we left Slack there amongst those spinning bicycle-wheels and pedals and went back into the mess and had another pint. Sergeant Slack was dead to the world for getting on for half an hour.

This episode had also come to the notice of the Flight Sergeant Disciplinarian and a report had followed.

Now the familiar verdict was given to me by the Flight Commander, namely that I was to be passed out but I really would have to become less aggressive on the ground, for my own good.

Once more I was on leave. This time, of course, I was waiting, as were all of us in this same situation, to hear what Squadron we would be posted to, and what our future marching-orders would be.

Again, at home, I was looked after very well by my parents and sister, my brother was at this time away in the Army in Italy or somewhere, until one morning a telegram arrived for me. My instructions were to report to 174 Squadron at Gravesend in Kent. I managed to make some enquiries about my new Squadron - 174 Squadron was a Hurricane Squadron.

CHAPTER FOUR

At the appointed date and time I made my way to Gravesend and found my Squadron. Here again I was lucky. The Squadron Commander, Squadron Leader McConnell, was a splendid chap, a typical sort of Senior Operational Officer.

My Flight Commander was a Flight Lt. Minal, a Canadian who took things fairly easy but obviously was a very good pilot. The rest of the Squadron were a mixture of Canadians, Australians and New Zealanders, and there were some of us English there as well!

I was not immediately accepted by the other Sergeant Pilots because I had not been into battle with them, as it were. They had been having a pretty rough time. They had converted to being 'Hurri-Bombers', which meant that they carried a couple of 500lb bombs, one under each wing. They had been involved in the Dieppe Show which was a bit of a disaster, whereby they had received some pretty heavy casualties, hence myself as one of the replacement pilots.

As I say, I was a bit lonely at first because, until I'd been bloodied in action, I wasn't really to be accepted. Nevertheless, we carried on practice-flying on Hurricanes for a while, just doing formations and general aerobatics and so on because the Squadron was waiting to be re-equipped with Hawker TYPHOONS.

Everyone was rather in awe of Typhoons because they were a prototype. They hadn't seen much service at all. They had just been in the experimental stages during which there had been several fatal accidents. I think that squadrons no. 56 and 266 were the earliest to have them.

Firstly, the Typhoon had had engine troubles and, secondly, it had a nasty habit of developing metal fatigue between the cockpit and the tail. With any violent movement or stress the tail would drop off and the pilot would hit the ground fairly hard - and that would be that.

Then came the day when the first of the Typhoons was delivered to us in April 1943. We all gathered round it and looked up at it. It really was, or certainly appeared to be, a monster of an aeroplane. It had an enormous nose with a 2,000 hp engine contained therein. A 2,000 hp Sabre engine. We had heard that it was capable of 400 mph and we had also been told that it was very heavy on controls. This was so different to the gentle Hurricane we were used to.

Stan Minal, my Flight Commander, had a go in it first. When he came down, he spoke to us and said that it was indeed a very heavy aeroplane to fly. Also, he said, that on take-off it had a yaw to starboard through torque, which meant that you had to take counter-action, but not too much or you would get into a swing and probably ground-loop. Briefly, it wasn't an easy aeroplane to fly and we were to take our turns in it to try it out, obviously solo.

My turn came and I can remember now going out on my own and staring at it and thinking, "I hope I can cope with this."

I climbed into the Typhoon and got the ground crew to help me start it up. I was just going to take off when Stan Minal came running up and shouted, "Hey, where are you going, Pete? You're not supposed to go yet. I wanted to give you some more details on it."

So I replied, "Well, I think I know what it's all about, Sir."

To which he said, "Oh, all right then. Off you go." And so I went to take off. It was just as he had said. I gave it the necessary amount of throttle to get up to take-off speed, and indeed it did start to swing from one side to the other, but I was able to counteract this. Mind you, I did make a rather ropey take-off but, nevertheless, I did get in the air.

I made a couple of circuits, found out where and how to operate the undercarriage, pitch control, flaps, etc. and brought it back-in fairly reasonably. Anyway, Stan was quite happy with me. He was sure that I was confident in handling it. I agreed that I was, and we went on from there.

Within the next month we'd been re-equipped with the Typhoons and our dear old Hurricanes had been taken away. We then moved base down to the South coast, in the first instance to Lydd on the Romney Marshes where we were billeted in tents on the camp. At this time there were three Squadrons of Typhoons there - ourselves and two others - forming a Wing, 121 Wing. We now came under 2nd Tactical Air Force. Obviously, the purpose of our existence was for us to be in on the invasion of the German-occupied continent.

We got ourselves settled in and I knew that my first operation was imminent. At this stage, we were to be fitted with two 500lb bombs, one under each wing, complete with our cannons, as well. The object of the operation was to attack enemy airfields in Normandy, such as Amiens, with a view to putting out the Luftwaffe and any resistance from them at such a time as we did make the invasion.

I don't think any pilot or any aircrew member ever forgets the details of his first operational trip. In my own case, it was early one morning when I was told that, along with the rest of the Squadron, I was going on a sortie.

We were taken in a truck along to a Briefing Room in the Lydd area, which was a Nissen hut. Here we were told that our target was such and such, what positions to take in the Flight, what the flak resistance was likely to be en route, and which direction we should approach our target from, etc.

There were twelve aircraft - three Flights of four, I recall - and our Squadron name was 'Crayfish'. The position that I was to be given was 'Crayfish Blue Four', which meant that I was going to be the last one in to the target. I vividly remember one of the other more experienced pilots saying that I shouldn't be put in that position as, without previous experience, it didn't give me much of a chance of getting out because all the flak would be really warmed up by then and I would really cop it! None of which added greatly to my confidence and, as we were trundled back in the same truck to join our aircraft, I began to have mixed feelings about the operation - whether I wanted to go or not. But, obviously, we had to go.

On these particular sorties, we would form up over the Romney Marshes, climb out over the Channel to about 5,000 feet, and then cross the enemy coast.

They would soon liven up to the fact that we were around, and would start shooting at us. You would then get flak-bursts all round you. Nevertheless, you pressed on to Amiens, which wasn't very far inland, and took up position.

We would attack in echelon formation, with me right on the end. The leader of the Squadron went in first. We sorted out the targets, such as Dispersal Units and aircraft standing about the place, dropped our bombs, pulled out of our dive, and then headed back towards the coast.

The flak was pretty heavy all the way from Amiens-Glissy to the coast, and by the time we got to the French coast it was really hot. This was light flak but, nevertheless, it was pretty uncomfortable and quite formidable.

As we crossed out over the coast, I saw two aircraft alongside me get hit and they, in fact, crashed into each other and they spiralled down tangled up together. So that was two of them gone. We could do nothing but make our way back to Lydd airstrip and make our report on what had happened.

It later transpired that the result of this raid was that we had put Amiens-G1issy aerodrome out of action, but at a cost of two pilots and two aircraft.

I had completed my first operational mission. The only happy thing about this was that I now truly became a member of the Squadron and was allowed to join my friends, comrades and fellow pilots in the local pubs and so on, and was generally accepted.

We carried out several trips similar to this from Lydd with the 500lb bombs, generally speaking on aerodromes. This went on for a while until it was getting near to wintertime, then we were moved away from Lydd, further down the coast to a satellite of Tangmere, Westhampnett, in Hampshire, where we were going to start operating in a rather different role.

In the place where the 500lb bombs had been, we had installed what were called drop-tanks. These were petrol tanks which would just about enable us to double our range so that we could go inland into enemy territory as far as Paris. But, of course, it did limit our firepower in that all we now had were four 20mm cannon. These could still cause plenty of damage though.

Our main targets now were enemy troop-trains and ammunition dumps, or opportunity targets and various targets given to us by the French Resistance.

Some of the opportunity targets were quite interesting. For instance, we might hear of a train going from A to B in France with Reich Marshal Goering, head of the Luftwaffe, supposedly on it, so you'd go down after it. I don't expect he was on it at all.

Sometimes you'd come across what were called 'Q' trains. This was a matter of attacking what you thought was a troop-train or maybe an ammunition-train, and then, all of a sudden, the sides would drop down and these trains would be full of anti-aircraft guns and the gunners would just shoot at you. We would just shoot back and then probably call it a day.

After the Germans, our secondary enemy was the weather. Our climate is very unpredictable, and we did experience considerable difficulty in completing some of our missions because of it.

A Squadron of us set out from Tangmere in November '43 when the weather was very bad. We headed out very low, narrowly avoiding the spire of Chichester Cathedral which was literally the same height as we were flying. We had been assured that the weather should clear after we got over the Channel so that we would be able to attack our target, which was again an enemy aerodrome.

We swung round and flew along the coast as far as our old friend Lydd, at which point we were to turn and head for the enemy coast. Cloud-level at this stage was under 1,000 feet. We turned towards the coast, all twelve of us, and as we went over the Channel, instead of the weather clearing, the cloud of mist came right down to sea level. We could see nothing ahead.

The Squadron leader decided to climb to gain height and try to get through this stuff, so we went into this cloud hoping at some stage of the game to come out through it. As I say, the weather was extremely unpredictable and we had been told that it was going to improve, instead of which it became absolutely diabolical.

We went into this cloud in formation, and it got darker and darker until it was pitch black. The only way to fly now was on instruments for, obviously, we could not fly visually. I dropped my eyes to my instrument-panel and, oh dear, the instruments had gone for a Burton! I'd got nothing except for my airspeed indicator, which was dropping fast.

The stalling-speed in a Typhoon is about 80mph, so when my speed got down to about 150, I was getting rather worried. If your airspeed drops, the thing to do is to push the stick forward to get the nose down to try to gain more speed. With full throttle on, this didn't work. The airspeed continued to drop. I thought I was going to get into a stall and from that into a spin from which there was no way you would ever recover.

Now, I'm not a religious person, but at the same time I'm not non-religious, but at that point I do remember thinking, "Oh, Christ! This is it."

Without my doing anything further, and this is quite true, the stick which I'd been trying to push forward, suddenly came back, and not of my own volition. The stick came back towards my stomach when I was very near to stalling-speed. It obviously pulled me back on to my back and the aeroplane into a loop, with two 500lb bombs on if you please!

The Typhoon was shuddering violently, and me with it, and all the muck was coming up out of the floor of the cockpit. It was still shuddering and spluttering when, suddenly, it seemed to just drop out of the loop, and I was now plummeting towards the sea, about 5,000 feet below me, I suppose. The airspeed was building up, so I just let the aircraft fly itself virtually. I got to a reasonable flying speed, I would guess about 250 knots, and came out at about 800 feet above the sea. I saw the breakers, pulled the stick back and just skimmed across the surface.

I called out a Mayday to base, which was received, and a reply came back ordering me to jettison the two 500lb bombs as it would have been even more dangerous to land with them. I flew back to Tangmere and touched down safely.

Really, this could be said to illustrate two things; one, that the weather was our enemy, and two, that perhaps Christ was on our side?

However, to return to our rather different role of using long-range drop-tanks where the bombs had been. To begin with these drop-tanks did give a fair amount of trouble. The principle in their use was to fly the extent of your outward journey on the drop-tanks, drop them, i.e. jettison them, and fly back on your main tanks. This in itself scared the Germans because they thought they were bombs falling.

When they were jettisoned, the drop-tanks should have sealed off from the main fuel-supply, but what was happening was that they weren't doing so properly, causing the main tanks aboard to leak from the wings. We lost a couple of pilots as a result of this malfunction and sure enough, it happened to me.

I was flying in the Paris area and I dropped my extra tanks just off the city and turned for home. I saw to my horror that the petrol was gushing out of my mains at the back of my wings as I tried to make it to the coast. Once at the coast, I had to make a quick decision. I'd got up to about 5,000 feet and, I remember, the engine was running a bit rough. I called out to the Squadron Commander back at base for advice. He couldn't really do anything only say that the ultimate decision had to be mine. I could either turn back into France, and probably get taken prisoner, or try to cross the Channel, which looked a bit cold. (It was November, of course.) I thought, well, I'll have a go.

The Squadron Commander then detailed my Flight Commander to nurse me back. He reckoned the best place, or the nearest point, to take me to was Beachy Head. That would make for the least amount of water for me to have to fly over.

As Beachy Head was looming up I had lost almost all my height and the engine was beginning to cut. It seemed rather like a scene from an American film, but this was reality. Somehow, I just skimmed the grass on our most famous suicide spot and got the aircraft down in one piece. Well, more or less in one piece.

From this incident they were able to examine my aircraft, one that had survived the fuel-loss fault, and determine the cause of the trouble that occurred when the drop-tanks were jettisoned. From this near disaster, some good came. The engineers re-modified the valve that had caused the problems on the drop-tanks and, fortunately, we were not to have this trouble any more.

In October 1943, to give us a little bit of variety, as if we needed it, they introduced rocket projectiles to us. These were 60lb warheads on rockets. We were to carry eight of them, four under each wing, in place of where the 500lb bombs had been, or alternatively the long-range tanks. These R.P's as we called them were fired from racks under each wing.

We had to go on a special training-course to learn how to use them. The main idea was to predetermine your angle of attack and the height at which you were going to release them, which was going to be pretty near the deck, and then just let 'em go. The force of letting all eight rockets go at once was enough to throw the Typhoon back. This was pretty scary at times. Remember, the Typhoon was twice as big as a Spitfire, and it weighed nearly seven tons when fully loaded!

There were a whole series of targets on the French coast to go after. Because we were carrying rockets now, once again our range was limited. Some of our targets were radar stations. This was in order to knock out enemy radar before the invasion, so they wouldn't know what the hell was going on when we were going over. Other targets were so-called 'Construction' or 'Noball' sites.

We really didn't know what these were, but obviously the powers that be did, which is fair enough because it didn't matter a damn to us except that we were supposed to do our best to knock 'em out. Which we did. But they really were very heavily defended.

It turned out that they were Doodlebug sites, constructed launching ramps in preparation to shoot off the V-1 flying-bomb towards this country. When we went in to attack 'a very important target' just inland from Cap Gris Nez, near Calais, we didn't know any of this. We were warned that it would be just about the most heavily-defended target that we'd ever gone for, and that we would be lucky to get back, but it was vital that we hit it.

As it happened, the weather clamped down and we were grounded but, as you can imagine, having a briefing like that we were in a rather shaky sort of state. And then it clamped down the next day, so again we couldn't get at it. And the following day.

Eventually, on the third day following our initial briefing, we took off and headed along the coast. From Lydd, we set our course and climbed to 5,000 feet towards Cap Gris Nez. As we approached - we were the third Squadron in - we could see the flak coming up at us, as had been predicted, fairly heavy, but we kept going.

I saw one or two of our aircraft going down. This was one of the times when you wished you hadn't joined the R.A.F. but, nevertheless, we pressed on, got to the right height, adjusted our rockets, made our attack, and did the best we could. I doubt if we obliterated the target, but we definitely had put it out of action for some time. The R.P.s had certainly done their stuff. We suffered some further casualties but, luckily, I got back from the mission all in one piece.

It was about this stage in operations that, by virtue of my good behaviour and air-experience, I had been commissioned. I was now Pilot Officer Peter Watson.

Again we were on the move. This time to Holmesly South, just near Herne Airport. It was the Spring of 1944, almost immediately prior to the invasion. At this time the most outstanding event in our day to day existence must have been the visit paid to us by General Eisenhower. This was partly out of his wanting to know what we were up to and partly as a morale booster for us.

Eisenhower was the most splendid person you can imagine. We had laid on a show for him, which was to attack a viaduct in France. Because we knew he would be listening to the Radio Transmissions between us, we wanted to make a good job of it.

We flew over and across the Channel and again we ran into heavy flak as we approached the target area. Not only that, but the weather conditions were absolutely ghastly. There was low cloud with just a few patches in between and we were weaving all over the place, partly to avoid the flak and partly

Peter Watson third from right front row 174 Squadon August 1943

Above: Hawker Typhoon 1B

Left to right recently
Commissioned Pilot Officers
Harry 'Junior' Markby, Peter
Watson, Eric Little 174 Squadron
Westhampnett Nov.1943

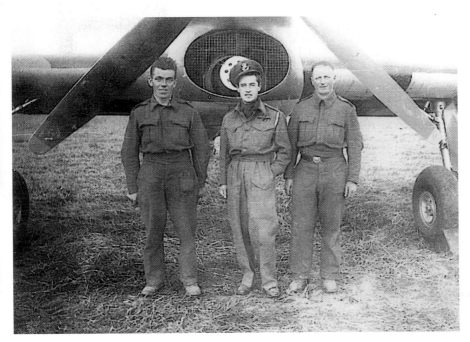

*Peter Watson (centre) with armourer and fitter B-5 Airfild Caen France
July 1944*

*Peter Watson's 'Vliegerkruis'
(Dutch D.F.C.) awarded 1945*

F/Lt Peter Watson RAFVR

Above: Peter Watson examines Typhoon cockpit at Shoreham Aviation Museum

Left: Peter Watson with Harvard Trainer Shoreham airfield mid 1990's

Below: From left to right Doug Oram, Peter Watson, Frank Wheeler, Jack Hodges, Ian Mallet, ex 174 Typhoon squadron reunion. Shoreham June 2000

to find a hole whereby we might see this wretched viaduct. General Eisenhower could obviously hear us screaming at each other over the R/T with all the various obscenities and general frustration.

Then, very quickly, two things came to my aid. One was my good luck and the other was my good eye. I was just weaving about over the target zone with flak coming up all around me when, suddenly, there was a hole in the cloud. The sun shone from above, right through the hole, as if spotlighting a picture - and there it was, the viaduct.

I yelled out that I'd got a visual contact, set my sights on it and screamed down towards it, pushing my rocket and cannon buttons at the same time and put a salvo in. This meant that my whole eight rockets and cannon shells fired in one go! I hit the viaduct right in the middle - absolutely clobbered it. I'm sorry to say, nobody else did, I was the only one.

I felt very proud as we returned to base. I'd hit the thing loud and clear and our Squadron's honour was intact, just from one chance sighting.

General Eisenhower was at our de-briefing. He said, "I heard you hit the target. Who was it that hit it? Who was it that got it so good?"

The Wing Commander replied, "It was Pilot Officer Watson, Sir."

So little Pilot Officer Watson was made to step forward, and General Eisenhower said, "Er...Congratulations, Mr. Watson - that was mighty nice shootin."

Which was a very good cue for another beer with a large whisky chaser. As I drank, I thought, " Here's to rocket projectiles!"

It was now May, just before D-Day. D-Day, the invasion of the Continental mainland, as we all know now, was June 6th, 1944.

We occupied our time by making ourselves useful in this period running up to D-Day by attacking, mainly in France, transport and German army convoys, railways and trucks. In fact, any sort of military target that moved. We were just building up and waiting for the go-ahead for D-Day. Of course, none of us knew what was actually going to happen on D-Day, but everyone was determined to win through and we realised that it was still going to be a pretty dicey business.

There were many preparations to be made. I remember I was told to take my car home, say goodbye to my parents, who

obviously knew that something big was going on, and then
return to my squadron at Holmesly South - to wait.

CHAPTER FIVE

The waiting and relative inactivity led, as you can imagine, to quite a bit of drinking. And in and around our own particular area, this applied not just to us, but to the locals as well. In fact, when on the evening of June 5th we were confined to camp, we all felt quite relieved. We were called up for a briefing and told that the show was definitely on for the following morning.

D-Day dawned. The sun rose and at 6 am we took off. We had a beautiful clear sky. With Holmesly South falling swiftly behind us, we purposefully swept over our own coast and across the Channel to search out our targets.

Suddenly, below us, a most breathtaking sight met our eyes. A fantastic armada of ships was approaching the enemy coast. You couldn't see the Channel for ships.

As we crossed the enemy coast our troops were just disembarking. There was fire all around. The flak was intense but there was absolutely no aerial resistance. This we had either previously knocked out or driven further inland.

Our targets were artillery posts and any troop concentrations we could hit. Anything to support our landing-forces. As soon as our ammunition was exhausted, we returned to base where we were de-briefed. We told everyone what the immediate situation was over there.

Winston Churchill had made one of his remarkable speeches which I'm sure gave us all such tremendous encouragement. We took some refreshment while our aircraft were being re-fuelled and re-armed ready to take off again.

Again and again we went over, steadily supporting our ground troops in any way possible. The following day, and the following day, and on and on. Ceaseless attacks on enemy communications, troop concentrations, trains, supply-lines, ammunition-supplies, lines of reinforcements to their front line, anything we could. This all went on just inland of the battle, or as we called it the 'bomb-line', with our people on one side of it, and theirs on the other.

On D-Day plus 5, we were told that we had made sufficient progress in France whereby our airfield construction units had been able to lay down airstrips for us. This meant we could now land in France and operate from there, saving the continuous trips over the Channel. It also gave us a lot more fuel, and consequently more range, and, most vital, more time to support our ground troops.

We packed all our gear in wing gunbays and so on, tents and all the equipment that we could fit in, even some in our cockpits, and on D-Day plus 5, we actually landed at an airstrip just on the coast side of Caen. This base was called B-5. All temporary airfields after the invasion of northern Europe were given the prefix B. B-1, B-2, etc.

Caen was a very heavily contested target, the Germans were really putting up a fight there. In fact, they weren't more than five miles away when we touched down in France. When the airstrip construction crews were busy laying down the strip they had been under constant shell attack from the Germans and we too were under constant fire as we put our tents up and prepared to make our operational trips.

It was now that all R.A.F. personnel in France were issued with British Army khaki battledress. Our Royal Air Force blue was too similar to the colour that the Germans wore and from the air we could be mistaken for Jerry and fired on by our own planes. Also, if any of our aircraft got shot down over enemy territory, we could be confused with the enemy as we made our way back towards Allied lines. All aircrew were also now armed with Smith and Wesson 45 revolvers.

At night now there was very little chance of grabbing any sleep because the German bombers were coming over to attack us on this rather thin line of coast that we had grabbed from them. The British ack-ack gunners made it look like some colossal firework display, and shrapnel from their exploding shells was fairly raining down on us. It was a pretty dodgy and noisy affair.

We soon managed to settle down to these somewhat rugged conditions of life. Our cooks were marvellous. They managed to supply us with meals out of the iron rations we were all on, supplementing these with local vegetables and anything else they could lay their hands on. They really did us proud in order to keep us going.

We continued with our daily sorties. Now, of course, without that Channel to cross, we could do a trip fully loaded with rockets, attack our targets - ground troops, artillery emplacements, etc. - and shunt straight back. The Germans were now twenty to thirty miles from us.

I think my shortest trip took only twenty minutes from taking off, attacking my target, returning to base, landing, re-fuelling, re-arming, and back in the air. What a difference!

And so it went on and on. As the days went by, our ground forces slowly but surely made their progress inland, and we helped them as much as we could by doing 'armed reconnaissance', as we called it, on the enemy side of the bomb-line. We would attack anything we thought opportune - convoys, communications, trains, etc. We also introduced, or rather it was introduced to us, a new form of warfare, which was called 'cab-rank' warfare. This involved direct Army/R.A.F. co-operation.

We would fly up and down the bomb-line and there would be an Army Bren-gun carrier right in the battlefield. He would locate a pocket of resistance from the enemy, give us a grid-reference on the map, which we had across our knees, and we would fly straight in and knock it out. He would be giving us these directives from his tank.

This was a most effective form of Army/R.A.F. co-operation. On one particular occasion, I recall, we were hard at it when our Army comrade suddenly stopped talking. We looked down and saw that the enemy had put him out of action.

I was to discover in recent years that much of the information, especially in the laying down of the bomb-line, was provided by a semi secret army regiment, General Headquarters Liaison Regiment, officially code-named Phantom, who would be in front of our forces as they went into battle. The bomb-line was a regularly up-dated line on our maps that stopped us from firing on our own forces as they advanced towards the Germans.

Phantom would also find and locate enemy troop movements, especially armour, and we would attack on this information.

We would sometimes be briefed by an Army officer, probably from Phantom, before missions into enemy territory, with the information coming from various resistance movements who were working with the S.A.S. The S.A.S. often had Phantom patrols with them providing their communication back to Army and Air Force H.Q's. I take my hat off to the boys of PHANTOM.

Andy and Sue Parlour have written a book entitled 'PHANTOM AT WAR' to be published soon by Ten Bells Publishing Ltd.

With the steady progress we were making our morale now inevitably began to improve, as did everyone else's.

Just a week after D-Day we were honoured with a visit from that great man, Prime Minister Winston Churchill. He'd obviously come to visit us, like General Eisenhower had, partly to see what was going on for himself, and partly to boost our morale.

Churchill treated us to one of his speeches. To us it was awe-inspiring, something fantastic. He seemed somehow to be speaking to each one of us individually, giving us the strength and determination to carry on the fight.

He came at tea-time. A Dakota had been sent over to the U.K. to pick up buns and cakes and things especially for this visit because he was expected to have tea with us before his own return to England.

Well, after his speech, we all traipsed over to the marquee on the border of the airstrip. There were two marquees there, one with the tea and buns and the other one, the mess tent, with the drinks or whatever was going.

Churchill pointed his stick at one marquee and asked the Group Captain, who was escorting him, "What's in there?"

He was told it was tea and buns. He didn't seem to go much on this and, pointing to the other, said, "What's in there?"

He was informed that that was the mess.

With a vigorous jab of his stick, he indicated that he was going into the mess tent, no doubt for a well deserved brandy and cigar. We were shuffled into the tea and buns tent.

Churchill was a great man, certainly the greatest leader this country has ever had. Possibly the greatest leader the world has ever had. He was most certainly a huge inspiration to all of us.

From B-5 we moved forwards to the Lille area of France where there was a proper aerodrome. Here we established that our ground forces, just ahead of us, were awaiting our next move. By now the Germans were well on the run, but what happened one night almost made me believe that they wanted to join us.

We were attacking a concentration of tanks. The Squadron and Wing were all involved in this one. We were right on the deck, firing our rockets and cannons, destroying these tanks most effectively, when I happened to look at the aircraft flying next to me. It was only a couple of hundred yards away when I noticed it had got black crosses on it! I instantly realised that it was not one of ours. It was, in fact, a Messerschmidt M.E.109 whose pilot had craftily infiltrated into our attacking force. He was attempting to shoot down the aircraft ahead of me. This was all happening at between 500 and 1000 feet.

There was only one thing for it. I wheeled over smartly onto his tail. He spotted me instantly and made a very quick turn to take evasive action away from me. I got my sights on him and pushed the button. The cannons didn't fire. Damn it! I'd used up all my ammunition.

So there we were, going round in circles, he no doubt absolutely terrified that I was going to shoot him down and wondering why the hell I didn't, and my rather wondering what on earth to do about it.

Luckily, he took some pretty smart evasive action, dived into a nearby cloud and disappeared. That was the one that got away. He could certainly handle that plane. I bore no animosity towards him at all, he was, after all, just an airman doing his job.

As I said, the Hun was on the run. It was now the end of August 1944, not yet three months since the invasion. We'd scored several successes, inflicting heavy casualties on the enemy, particularly at the Falaise Gap, just south of Caen, where we really massacred the German Seventh Army as they tried to retreat.

We had to do this because if we had allowed them to retreat and re-muster then they would have been able to fight another day. Fifty thousand Germans were taken prisoner in that mid-August battle.

At the same time, our ground forces had sustained some heavy losses and we ourselves had had casualties, several of them pilot friends of mine who had got shot down and had had to be replaced. But that was the way of the war. By now, however, we were obviously on the winning side and were advancing into what had been enemy-held territory, going in towards the Belgian border.

We'd been so much engaged all this time that we'd had very little 'social' life, shall we say. Of course, whenever we had the opportunity we would go into a local village or into a town, such as Lille, and sort out the estaminets and the 'madamoiselles', which was all quite fun, but there wasn't enough of it. There was too much war. But we were to have our chances later though when, from Lille, we advanced to an airfield just outside Antwerp. Now we did see some social life because we were able to go into the city.

We continued our constant operational sorties against the enemy, but were not at Antwerp very long before moving on to Vokel, which was just outside Eindhoven. Here we were allowed some leave, local leave that is, 48hr. passes. I remember the occasion they allowed us the use of an Auster light reconnaissance plane for transport purposes to get us on leave.

Off we went then, Eric Little, Junior Markby, both Australians, and myself, flying off to Antwerp. We had a pretty good leave with all the booze and all the girls and all that.

We were due to fly back to Vokel early on the Monday morning. Well, in the dim dawn we were, shall we say, in a rather hazy state. We hadn't had any breakfast so we thought we'd buy something to eat on the way back in the Auster. All we managed to find to buy were some tomatoes. So we bought them and got aboard the Auster and off we went.

Junior was flying us back to base, pretty low, in fact it was almost at ground level. Anyway, I was sitting in the back of the aeroplane and none of us noticed that we were going a bit off course, but we obviously must have been because we suddenly heard some cracking and banging noises.

Well, we looked over the side and there were these chaps in grey uniforms and steel helmets with rifles sort of irately shooting at us. So, not to be outdone, I opened the cockpit window and instructed the two Australians to throw our tomatoes at these offensive Germans, which we did.

Now this Auster was only going about 70mph and there we were chucking these tomatoes at these rather amazed Germans, they must have thought they were grenades, which severely put them off their aim, because they didn't hit us once and we were able to get back to Vokel in one piece. Needless to say, we did not make any report on this affair.

I had another good friend when we were in the invasion forces based at Vokel. His name was 'Tiny' Irwin, a most marvellous chap, and we were great mates, going around together a great deal. He was an ex-Indian Army officer, now a Flight Lt. We must have appeared a rather strange contrast because he was 6'6"tall and I was only 5'6"tall, but we were great friends.

We went on a show one day and were attacking a troop train and some tanks when 'Tiny' got hit. We were circling round at the time and I saw him crash land. He got his aeroplane down and I saw him running away from it towards some woods to escape being captured. This was fairly near the bomb-line, but

I do know he got away from his aircraft and was not killed. Automatically when this occurs and someone does not return, a telegram is sent by the Adjutant of the Squadron to the next of kin to inform them that someone is missing.

Almost immediately after this, while attacking an enemy troop-train, I myself got very badly hit by flak. A shell came right up through the mainplane. It must have come up between the aileron wires, there was just room for it to, and exploded beside the cockpit. Shrapnel whizzed into my cockpit. One piece actually took the goggles right off my forehead, just grazing the bridge of my nose, and disappeared out the other side. However, the aeroplane was still flyable and I was still able to fly it, so I called out to the Flight Commander that I had been hit on the head.

He came back, rather callously I thought, with, "Well what d'you expect me to do about it?"

So I said, "Well, I want to go home."

So I was escorted back to base. The aircraft, as I said, was just about flyable, but rather difficult to manoeuvre. I reached Vokel and called out that I was going to make an emergency-landing. Not knowing whether the undercarriage or flaps or anything else had been shot away, I did a dummy-run over the Control Tower. They peered up at me and announced that my undercarriage was down all right.

I made one last circuit and managed to bring her in without any further trouble and taxied back. Everyone looked at me and the aeroplane in some amazement as they didn't realise how it could still fly with the hole in the wing and the hole in the cockpit, and on top of everything I'd dented my nose.

After the debriefing, I didn't fly for a day or two. The Squadron Leader, Squadron Leader Pitt Brown, came up to me and said, "Well, we've patched up your aeroplane for you."

I said, "Thank you very much, Sir."

He went on, "We thought it might make rather a break for you to fly it back to England and get it replaced."

I replied, "Okay, Sir. Thank you very much."

As I made my preparations to leave, it suddenly occurred to me that I might kill two birds with one stone.

So I paid a visit to the Adjutant and said, "Look, I'm going back to the U.K. and we have now heard that 'Tiny' Irwin is among our own troops, so why don't I tell his wife that he is, in fact, safe and well and has not been captured by the enemy or killed or anything like that?"

We had heard by now that 'Tiny' had successfully got himself over the bomb-line and got in amongst our own men. With communications as they were, it could well be weeks before 'Tiny's' wife heard the news, and she would still be thinking that 'Tiny' could have been killed. The Adjutant readily agreed.

So my XPH, that was my aircraft number, with metal plates holding it together so that it was at least flyable after a fashion, with me aboard, took off. We went along the coast, intending to turn and cross on a heading for the U.K. What I'd forgotten was that Dunkirk, an area I suppose about the size of Brighton, was still a pocket of German resistance.

When I flew over it, they shot at me! I took a bit of evasive action, which in its present state XPH wasn't really up to, and noticed I was running a bit short on fuel, so I decided to make for Hawkinge, in Kent, which was the nearest aerodrome for me.

The weather conditions were very poor and the cloud-base was down to about 1,000 feet, but I recalled that I had a W.A.A.F. girlfriend at Hawkinge, which greatly encouraged me to press on. So I called out over button 'D' that I was going to make an emergency-landing at Hawkinge, flew in and plonked her down. Then sorted out my W.A.A.F. girlfriend for that evening and night.

The next morning, feeling much more like my old self, I was supposed to proceed with XPH down to Thorney Island, near Portsmouth. The Fitter Sergeant was really rather unwilling to pass the aeroplane as flyable, but I finally persuaded him to let me go on.

I got along in a westerly direction as far as Gatwick and the weather really clamped down again. Of course, Gatwick was only about five miles from my home at Redhill so, naturally, I thought to myself, "I'll plonk this clapped-out Typhoon down here and go home." I promised to come back for her as soon as the weather cleared, which would probably be the next day, and got on a train to Redhill.

My parents were delighted to see me, and I them. I remembered my promise and called up 'Tiny's' wife that same evening. I told her the good news, that 'Tiny' was not in enemy hands, and she was so overcome that she couldn't speak, so I told her to get herself a drink and phone me back on my number in about five minutes. This she did and I was able to convince her that 'Tiny' was indeed OK. This was one of my pleasanter memories and indeed one of my happiest times.

Well, the next day the weather was still very poor, so there was no way I could get the Typhoon down to Thorney Island, with it being in such a poor condition anyway. In the end I took a train down there, leaving old XPH for some unfortunate pilot from Ferry Command to pick up at some later date.

At Thorney Island I picked up my replacement aircraft. I stayed there overnight and, when the weather cleared sufficiently, flew my brand new Typhoon back to Vokel, in Holland. My new Typhoon was also numbered XPH, to replace my old one, of course. And it was straight back onto operational sorties. Our first target on my return was an aerodrome right in Germany itself. It was the first time that any fighter-bomber or fighter aeroplane had got in as far as that over Germany. I remember at the briefing, we were told that this was to teach the Luftwaffe that they were now vulnerable to rocket-bearing Typhoon attacks from us.

We took off from Vokel, climbed, and crossed the Reichswald, an enormous expanse of forest, more distance to cross over than the Channel had been. Then we formed up over our target and made our attack. There was considerable ack-ack fire, as can be imagined, for the aerodrome did hold enemy aircraft. We destroyed some of them as they stood there on the ground, along with some nearby hangars and dispersal units of theirs, then got away smartly and returned to Vokel.

Next day we received a return visit from the Luftwaffe, who were obviously rather angry about us going in as far as their base. They had jet aircraft at this stage of the war, something which we had never heard about before, and, in rather an unfriendly way, dropped anti-personnel bombs on us. These were rather nasty things which exploded just above the ground and hurt you badly if they hit you. There were several casualties, some fatal.

Cowering in a slip-trench I heard one wag say, "And that was to teach us that we are not invulnerable from the Luftwaffe."

But that was the way things went, and I think we did well to get away with that one.

In mid-September, we heard that there was to be some British invasion force coming to drop by parachute and gliders into the Netherlands and to make a great advance towards Germany. This was confirmed one morning when we saw, flying in our direction, an enormous fleet. Squadron upon Squadron of gallant gliders being pulled by Dakotas headed, as we later found out, for the Arnhem area, whereby they were going to capture the river bridges and destroy the enemy. This, if it had worked, would have shortened the war by some considerable time.

Our job was to support, not so much the airborne forces there, but our main ground forces who were trying to get through to support them. I later found out that we were following up a column of the Irish Guards. Unfortunately, the wretched weather again hampered us considerably. We were flying below 500 feet, desperately trying to find our targets; German tanks and their main forces, who were stopping our main forces getting through to our airborne troops.

Once again, in appalling weather, my incredible luck came to our rescue. We were frantically trying to locate a triangular-shaped wood, signalled to us as a target by the Dutch Resistance, because it contained hidden under cover a number of German anti-tank gun troops. They were holding up our main forces from getting through to our lads.

We searched and searched but no way could we find the wood, or them, and we were, in fact, recalled to base.

In the same moment as we got the recall, there, just over my wing-tip, was this triangular-shaped wood. Thinking to myself that as I was there I might as well clobber it, I made four runs on it, that's four sets of two rockets, at tree-top height and then I let them have all my cannon. I really did hit it, loud and clear.

From later reports from the Dutch Resistance, we heard that there was nobody left alive in the wood.

I returned to base through a lot of enemy flak and, when I landed, found I'd sustained quite a lot of flak-damage to my aircraft, and also there were bits of tree from this wood still stuck in my radiator. Nevertheless, I again got back safely. The battle at Arnhem proceeded, but, I'm afraid, to our disaster.

At a later date, I did have the signal honour to be decorated by Prince Bernhard of the Netherlands on behalf of Her Majesty, Queen Wilhelmina, with the Vliegerkruis. This, the Dutch Flying Cross, I received for my various efforts in the Arnhem operation, and I am very proud of that recognition. I travelled to the Dutch Embassy in the West End's Portland Place to receive my medal and citation on the 31st July, 1945.

Peter Watson's citation:

I, WILHELMINA, BY THE GRACE OF GOD, QUEEN OF
THE NETHERLANDS, PRINCESS OF ORANGE-NASSAU,
etc. etc. etc.

on the recommendation of Our Ministers of War and for
Foreign Affairs, dated July 17, 1945, Section L O Nr.4;
HAVE APPROVED AND ORDERED

To award the 'Vliegerkruis' to:

Flying Officer P.R.WATSON

for:

Distinguishing himself during the operations near Arnhem
from September 17 to 25, 1944, by deeds of initiative,
courage and perseverence and showing, in every respect,
an uncommon devotion to duty and a great tenacity of purpose.

Our Ministers of War and for Foreign Affairs are in charge,
each for his own part, of the execution of this decree, copy
of which shall be sent to the chancellor of the
Netherlands Orders of Knighthood.

het Loo, July 31, 1945.
(sgd.) WILHELMINA

THE MINISTER OF WAR
(sgd.) J.MEYNEN

THE MINISTER OF FOREIGN AFFAIRS
(sgd.) VAN KLEFFENS

For translation and true copy:
(sgd.) L.C.RIETVELD

Soon after this it was decided that I should be sent back to
England on leave, for a rest. I was delighted. So off I went back
home again on leave to await further instructions.

These instructions came in their usual telegram form, telling
me that I was to be sent back up to where I'd first come from,

where I'd done my training on Hurricanes, only this time, I was to be an Instructor on Typhoons and a Test Pilot, which I was most happy to do. So I proceeded up north again to Millfield, near Alnwick, rather a more mature sort of person than when I had left it.

It was now my job to be an Instructor there, rather than a pupil. I really quite enjoyed the part I was playing. The only drawback was that the Typhoons were rather beat-up because they obviously weren't the top-grade aeroplanes that were needed over on the Front.

I also had to test-fly Typhoons, and that was a rather more precarious sort of business. I don't know if you could call it a rest, but it certainly was a change to war.

At Millfield I had managed to find myself a lady companion, a gorgeous little redhead W.A.A.F. We used to drink together and go out together. It was her main ambition to fly. She had never flown, and, being a W.A.A.F. she thought she ought to fly, at least once. So I said that perhaps I might be able to arrange something.

I knew I had to test-fly a Typhoon the very next morning, so I arranged for her to go behind an empty Dispersal shed at the bottom of the runway and told her to look out for me. I told her the number of my aircraft and that, when I got to the bottom of the runway ready for take-off, where no-one should see us, she should run over to the plane. I'd have the canopy open and she would jump into the cockpit with me.

Now both of us were fairly small, or else this would not possibly have worked. As it was, the only way that this was practical, was for her to jump in and face backwards, straddling my lap! Thus, she would be looking backwards and I would be able to look forwards over her shoulder to see where I was going and under her arm to see the instruments. In this position we gaily took off.

This was great fun. She seemed to be enjoying the flight immensely, particularly the position we were flying in, and it really was most stimulating. Especially when we went over a couple of air-pockets! In fact, I think this ought to have gone in the Guiness Book of Records, although they probably don't include the sort of thing that we were doing, even if it was at 5,000 feet.

I got her down, I mean back on the ground, she jumped out and scarpered behind another Dispersal hut, and we got away with it.

So, although this was a feature of Typhoon flying that I had not been specifically requested to test out that morning, I feel I can safely recommend the Typhoon as a very good high-flying substitute for the back seat of a car.

I was testing out HAWKER TEMPESTS later on when something else happened, but not in quite such a successful manner. I got into one, the successor to the Typhoon, having signed Form 700 which says that everything is OK and the aircraft has been checked out and all that. I taxied out, took off, and started climbing. At only about 200 or 300 feet, I suppose, the engine cut out on me!

There were two alternatives open to me. I could crash-land, straight ahead, or I could turn around and try to get the Tempest back on to the aerodrome. I decided on the latter.

Making what a motorist would call a U-turn, but with a spluttering aero-engine that there was only a little bit of life left in, I got the wheels and flaps back down again and landed downwind. That's 180 degrees in the opposite direction to which I'd taken off from. I got it down safely, all in one piece.

Well, I thought what a clever chap I was. The operator in the Control Tower thought so too. He said, "Jolly good show."

Unfortunately, when the Engineering Officer got hold of the aeroplane to see why it had packed up, it seems I'd taken off with very little fuel in it. It hadn't been re-fuelled, although it was supposed to have been.

Of course, as captain of the aircraft, I should have checked it and I hadn't. So I was held up on a charge for this, as was the airman who was supposed to have put the petrol in. We were both had up before the Commanding Officer.

He told me that I was being given a reprimand and an endorsement on my log-book. Another red endorsement! The C.O. angrily explained that if I'd been killed, as I could have been, the airman who should have put the petrol in, would have been up on a manslaughter charge.

My answer to this was, "Well, Sir, if I had been killed, I don't think I would have been too worried about that!"

This did not improve the C.O's temper. Anyway, the airman got away with a good rocket and a reprimand, and I got away with a reprimand and a red endorsement in my log-book.

All in all, it was very good fun up at Millfield, doing this test-flying and instruction. Especially all the larks we used to get up to!

While I was at Millfield the long years of war finally came to an end, so I never did have to return to the cut and thrust of air warfare.

I remained at this Northumberland airfield until I was posted to North Weald Airfield, near Epping in Essex. At North Weald, one of the Battle of Britain fighter airfields, I was privileged to serve under one of the war's greatest heroes, Group Captain Douglas Bader, later Sir Douglas, who had only recently returned to Britain from Germany where he had been a prisoner-of-war for four years. Here I was promoted to Flight Lieutenant and made Section Controller, but I was not to end my service days here, for I was then posted to Martlesham Heath, near Ipswich, Suffolk, to complete a Ground Control Intercept Course.

I was de-mobilised from the Royal Air Force in October 1946. After a couple of years in various occupations, I applied for a job with the Whitbread Brewery in their City of London office, which I was lucky enough to get. In the fifteen years that I was there, I rose from the position of clerk to district manager, retiring in 1963.

Thinking back, perhaps the worst part of the war was not the actual operations, but the dreadful anticipation, thinking of what might happen to you when you were confronted with the various situations which were bound to come. They did come. Time and time again. It was a matter of surmounting them, of overcoming your fear. Fear which anyone, any human person, must feel when they think they are facing probable death.

This was the worst part.

CHAPTER SIX

FLAK - Enemy anti-aircraft fire directed at us from the ground.

Probably one's first experience of flak was as you were nearing, or were over, the coast of France, approaching your target area, when the enemy anti-aircraft gunners would realise you were around and start shooting at you.

In the first instance you would see these small clouds of smoke, feathery smoke, usually light-coloured. We would, in Typhoons, be at about 5,000 feet and flying in 'open' formation. This 'open' formation meant the opposite of 'close' formation. In other words, we would leave a lot more actual room or airspace between each of the aircraft flying in the formation. This would give each aircraft enough room to manoeuvre as, at 5,000 feet, you would not be directly set on your target merely flying towards the target area. At that height, you could take evasive action from the flak.

Taking evasive action meant you would dive, weave, i.e. turn to port (left), or starboard (right), and keep in motion rather than flying in a straight line, this to generally confuse the ack-ack, or anti-aircraft, gunners or their direction-finding equipment.

Normally you wouldn't hear the flak, but if it was very close you would hear its very familiar but indescribable noise as the flak shells burst around you, giving off the little puffy clouds of smoke I described earlier. The sound of this noise was a kind of 'rrrumph'. If you could hear it, it meant that the flak was bursting very, very close to your aircraft. Remember, we had the noise of a 2,000-plus horse power Napier 'Sabre' aircraft engine and we were flying in an enclosed cockpit wearing a flying-helmet which covered our ears, with possible radio bursts coming through our headphones as well, plus the vibration from the engine. Therefore, if you heard the flak over all this, it had to be very close, lethally close.

I'm told that the 'one that got you' was the one you didn't hear, and you didn't know much about it either if it was a direct hit. I suppose you would just be obliterated.

If you actually had time to study the flak-bursts, they were that fluffy sort of powdery smoke with, inside, a ball of fire where the shell had exploded and from which shrapnel would fly out at enormous speed, hopefully not towards your aeroplane. It was unlikely that you would receive any damage from this unless you got a direct hit. So provided you didn't, you should get away with it.

I have been describing medium flak.

Now shrapnel was small pieces of metal thrown out by the exploding shell. Again these could be lethal if they were jagged and came at you at enormous speed and whizzed about alarmingly.

As you were approaching your target you could dive and weave about because you hadn't got your sights set on anything. But, once you'd committed yourself to your dive down to attack a target on the ground, having therefore set your sights and your fuses, and with your eye on the target, then you could not take any further evasive action because obviously it would spoil your aim. So you just had to go through the stuff. Firstly through medium-sized flak and then through light flak, which was tracer bullets, or tracer shells, which were inflammatory. These would be directed towards you from the ground. If they hit you, you could burst into flames, which for us was not a very happy thought. But, as I say, once you were committed to your target, you just had to go on and do the job, press the button and unleash your rockets.

My own reaction to this was as follows. My main object was to hit the target and get away, and get out of it as best I could and glad to be still alive. That was my first reaction. My second reaction was that if I saw one of my fellow pilots get hit, or shot down, then I would think "Oh, hell! Poor old Charlie," or whoever. My next thought would be, rather selfishly, for my own survival, and 'There but for the Grace of God go I'. And then I would get out of it as safely as I could and head for home.

Ideally, when attacking, I would prefer to unload all my rockets in one go, lessening my chances of getting hit or brought down by the flak. But, as when I was attacking the 'triangular wood' pinpointed by the Army and Dutch Resistance as having to be hit, I would quite often have to fire my eight rockets in pairs, thus necessitating four runs at the same target. Then, of course, I would have to contend with this flak four times on the trot!

Obviously one was apprehensive of flak. It was unavoidably there to get you, to destroy you and your aircraft, but another purpose of flak was to distract you from hitting your target or getting to your target, to unnerve you so that your aim would not be good and you would either miss your target or not even get there.

I've never spoken about this before, or discussed it with any other airman to discover whether their reactions were the same, but in these flak situations a physical phenomenon used to occur with me. An unnatural calm would come over me. Instead of distracting me the flak would give me added concentration. Every move I made with the Typhoon, like setting my sights, putting the fuses on, adjusting my angle of dive, throttlesetting, pitch-control, and that sort of thing, was done in a complete unnatural sort of calm, almost as if I was another person. Although I knew the flak was around, I would ignore it. You had to ignore it. It was no good, because there was a bit of flak around, saying to yourself, "Oh, that's enough of this, I'm gonna go home." You knew you'd got to carry on to the target and clobber it. As I say, I've never really thought about it before but it was an extraordinary business. I found when I was in any other danger, when I'd come to a crisis or near-crisis, that this calm would come over me which enabled me to overcome any fear that I had, and I could carry on with the job.

CHAPTER SEVEN

THE HAWKER TYPHOON VARIANTS.

1. F.18/37 R-Type (TORNADO) : One 1,760 H.P. (1313kW) Rolls-Royce Vulture II engine. Replaced in 1941 by: One 1,980 H.P. (1477 kW) Rolls-Royce Vulture V engine.

At first fitted with no armament, but then with 12 x .303 Browning machine-guns in the wings.

Maximum speed: 398 mph/640.5 kph at 23,000 ft/7010 m. Climb to 20,000 ft/6095 m. in 8 mins 25 secs. Service ceiling 34,900 ft/10640 m.

Weight: Empty - 8,377 lb/3800 kg. Laden (max t/off weight) - 10,668 lb/4839 kg.

Span: 41 ft.ll in/12.78 m.

Length: 32 ft 10 in/10.00 m.

Wing area: 283 sq.ft./26.29 sq.m.

There were two of these prototypes built.

2. F.18/37 (TORNADO) - Centaurus: One 2,210 H.P.(1649kW) Bristol Centaurus CE 4S radial engine driving a 4-blade propellor.

There was one of these prototypes built.

3. F.18/37 (TORNADO) - R-Type : One 1,980 H.P.(1477kW) Rolls-Royce Vulture V inline engine. Armed with 12 machine-guns.

Three of these (out of an order for 595) were built. Only one was flown, largely by Rotol in the development of contra-rotating propellor units.

4. F.18/37 N-Type (TYPHOON) : One nominally rated 2,055 H.P.(1533kW) Napier Sabre I engine. (Actually putting out less power)

At first fitted with no armament, but then with 12 x .303 Browning machine-guns.

The first prototype, P5212, built in March 1940, reached 410 mph/660 kph.

The second prototype, P5216, built in October 1940, reached 406 mph/653 kph.

There were two of these prototypes built.

5. HAWKER TYPHOON F1A : The initial production TYPHOON model. One 2,055 H.P. (1533kW) Napier Sabre I engine or One 2,180 H.P. (1626kW) Napier Sabre IIA engine.

Armament: 12 x .303 Browning machine-guns.

Length: 31 ft.10 in./9.70 m.

Height: 14 ft.10 in./4.52 m.

About 105 of these TYPHOON F1A's were built.

6. HAWKER TYPHOON F1B : The later production TYPHOON model. (with bubble canopy) One 2,200 H.P. (1641kW) Napier Sabre IIB engine or   One 2,260 H.P.(1686kW) Napier Sabre IIC engine.

Armament: 4 x 20 mm. Hispano cannon with
            either 2 x 500 lb./227 kg. bombs
            or 2 x 1,000 lb./454kg. bombs
            or 8 x 60 lb./27 kg. rocket projectiles

Length: Length 31 ft.ll 1/2 in./9.74 m.

Height : 15 ft.4 in./4.67 m.

About 3,210 of these TYPHOON FlB's were built.

7. HAWKER TYPHOON FR1B : Armed with only two Hispano cannon and various camera installations.

About 60 of these FRlB's altogether. All were conversions of other variants.

ORIGINS/BEGINNINGS/DEVELOPMENT/PRODUCTION

Air Ministry specification F.18/37. Main requirements sorted out early 1938. It was a product of the design team of Sydney Camm, at Kingston, Surrey, and was originally intended as a Fighter-Interceptor/Air combat Fighter.

It had problems with the engines used, the Rolls-Royce Vulture, the Bristol Centaurus and the Napier Sabre. Performance proved inferior to design intentions and requirements. It killed many pilots through a variety of causes not least the structural shortcomings in the rear fuselage.

In its favour were its sturdiness, its high speed and manoeuverability at low altitude and its supremacy in a ground-attack role.

Original armament intended by Hawker to be 12 x .303 Browning machine-guns, but the Air Ministry insisted on heavier calibre 20 mm. Hispano cannon.

The Camm design was conceived in two engine versions: 'N' - Napier Sabre. 'R' - Rolls-Royce.

In early 1938, 4 prototypes were ordered : two 'R'-type, to be given the name 'TORNADO' and two 'N'-type, to be called the 'TYPHOON'.

TORNADO's Vulture engine: basically 2 sets of V-12 Peregrine cylinder blocks arrayed in 'X' design round a common crankcase.

TYPHOON's Sabre engine: unconventional, its 24-cylinder engine was fitted with sleeve valves and arranged as two horizontally-opposed 12-cylinder engines one above the other, the two crankshafts driving a common reduction gear at the front. Both had water/glycol cooling. Both gave about 2,000 H.P.(1492kW)

The basic aircraft, TORNADO & TYPHOON, were the same except for the engines.

The fuselage structure was assembled by bolting or riveting steel tubes together, with gusset plates to reinforce the joints, and mountings at the front for the 2,000 H.P. engines. Though of aluminium-alloy, the inner wing was also a strong truss structure whose strength was augmented by its unusual thickness - thicker even than the wing of the HURRICANE, which was, at that time, in full production at the main Hawker works at Kingston, Surrey, and the new factory at Langley, Slough.

Unlike the HURRICANE, the F.18/37 had a semi-monocoque stressed-skin rear fuselage & outer wings. Ailerons and elevators had metal skin and the rudder was of fabric. An unusual feature was that the tailplane was in front of (clear of) the rudder.

The main landing gear had very wide track and retracted inwards outboard of the fuselage. It was hydraulic, as was the tail-wheel and split flaps. The cockpit had a 'car-door' type door on each side.

The first TORNADO, P5219, was built at Kingston, and flown at Langley by P.G.Lucas on 6th October ,1939. It had B-type (red & blue) roundels, it had 2 sets of exhaust stubs at each side of the nose, and a radiator under the belly.

Soon afterwards, Hawker received an order for 1,000 of the new fighters; 500 to be TORNADOS, 250 to be TYPHOONS, and the other 250 to be decided upon when it was known which engine was superior. Early on, the TORNADO had bad airflow round the radiator at high speed, and before the end of 1939 the P5219 was given the 'chin' radiator like that already chosen for the TYPHOON.

The first TYPHOON, P5212, was flown by P.G.Lucas from Langley on 24th February,1940. It was doped green above and silver below, with regular red/white/blue roundels. It was expected to reach 464 mph/747 kph. but the engine was unreliable. On 9th May, 1940, the fuselage broke aft of the cockpit, and P.G.Lucas had to make a forced landing.

Hawker, already mass-producing HURRICANES, were too pressed to be able to manufacture the TORNADO/TYPHOON order, so the TORNADO was assigned to Avro, and the TYPHOON to Gloster. Both were sister-firms in the Hawker Siddeley group.

In 1941, after numerous changes and refinements, both aircraft seemed ready for production.

The changes were a larger fin/rudder, wheel-well doors hinged first to leg-fairings then to the wing-roots, wings modified to fit for four cannon, extra windows aft of the canopy and a separate air inlet above the front cowling (TORNADO).

But the most worrying feature was the disastrous behaviour of both engines. Eventually Hawker was allowed to fit a TORNADO with a Bristol Centaurus, and this TORNADO, HG 641, flew on 23rd October, 1941. By this time the entire Vulture engine programme had collapsed, and with it the TORNADO. Just one single production machine, R 7936, flew from Avro's aerodrome at Woodford, Essex, in August 1941.

The Bristol Centaurus TORNADO flew better, more quietly, and more reliably. It was clearly the fastest. The TYPHOON was supposed to be capable of 464 mph/747 kph, but was only reaching 400 mph/644 kph The TORNADO, fitted with the Centaurus engine, was reaching 421 mph/677.5 kph, faster than any other fighter in the world at that time. With proper development it would have gone faster.

Air Marshal Wilfrid Freeman, in charge of procurement for the R.A.F., very much disliked Bristol radial engines, and he killed off the programme. In July 1942, Sydney Camm succeeded in fitting a Centaurus engine into a thin-wing TYPHOON II, later called the TEMPEST, but Air Marshal Freeman ordered it taken out again. This Centaurus TEMPEST was kept grounded until August 1943, thus seriously delaying the one really successful fighter of the F.18/37 family, which led to the post-war FURY and SEA FURY. Instead, Hawker had to struggle on with the most unreliable Sabre.

Production TYPHOONS began to appear slowly from 27th May, 1941, when R 7576 flew from the Gloster works at Hucclecote in Gloucestershire. Hawker only built 15 TYPHOONS, the first, R 8198, flying in November 1941.

About 100 early aircraft were TYPHOON 1As, with 12 Browning machine-guns, all the rest being TYPHOON 1Bs with 4 x 20mm cannon. Most of the cannon barrel projected well out of the wing's leading edges looking very aggressive.

Studies were made of long wing-span and clipped TYPHOONS and various other additions e.g. 1 or 2 turbo superchargers. But the only trial installations flown were the A1 Mk.VA with radar, and the FR.1B with various camera fits and only the outer cannon. About 60 of the FR versions were delivered.

THE HAWKER TYPHOON IN SERVICE WITH THE R.A.F.

The TYPHOON arrived at Duxford, (No.56 Sqn.), in late September 1941.

The Sabre engine ran 'like a sewing machine' when it worked, but it still proved extremely unreliable. The overhaul period was 25 hours. Visibility for the pilot was bad and performance, especially the climb and at height, was nowhere near up to, say, the Spitfire IX. The big TYPHOON fighter was rated in a dogfight as way inferior to an early Focke-Wulf 190.

Many TYPHOONS were lost, with some pilot fatalities, due to the tail falling off. It took, believe it or not, until near the end of the war to discover that the cure for the tail falling off lay quite simply in changing the elevator balance masses. Elevator flutter continued to cause problems for the pilots, and more and more metal reinforcing plates were added around the rear fuselage to keep the tail on.

A problem with the Napier Sabre engine soon became evident. A fatal accident in November 1941 caused this type of TYPHOON to be grounded for more than a month while tests were carried out. It turned out that the engine produced excessive amounts of carbon monoxide exhaust fumes which found their way into the cockpit. This had caused fatalities amongst other pilots. When it was discovered that this was the problem, modifications were made to the exhausts and the cockpit sealing. The defect was never fully remedied and all pilots were instructed to put on their oxygen mask as soon as they got into the cockpit and to keep it on until they had completed their flight.

In the period 1942-43, Air Staff and Ministry of Aircraft Production all but cancelled the TYPHOON. A young pilot with 609 Squadron, Roland Beamont, argued persuasively to keep the TYPHOONS on. Beamont was later to become one of the world's most famous test-pilots. The TYPHOON was not cancelled, Gloster continued building it, and Roland Beamont himself made 56 offensive sorties over enemy Europe, mostly by night.

The TYPHOON became successful as a destroyer of low-level flying enemy raiders. By late 1942, it became clear that the TYPHOON was ideally suited to ground-attack.

Successful trials with long-range drop-tanks were made, though when put into service, these too accounted for more pilot fatalities and crashes until Peter Watson of 174 Squadron, successfully limped back to Friston, on the Sussex coast, with his TYPHOON in one piece, which enabled evaluation tests of the problem which led to a cure.

In tests, 500 lb bombs, 1000 lb bombs, and 8 x 60 lb/27 kg rocket projectiles were fired from rocket-rails under the wing. These tests were all carried out successfully. This meant that the TYPHOON's role was switched from a fighter to a ground-attack aircraft. The whole of the R.A.F. TYPHOON complement was assigned to the newly-formed 2nd Tactical Air Force to attack European ground targets and enemy shipping.

In 1943, the TYPHOON had the black and white stripes (later the Invasion markings) painted on to prevent identification confusion with the German Fw 190. U.S. pilots were unaware of the TYPHOON to begin with and tried to shoot them down. At the same time, P-47 THUNDERBOLTS in the U.S. were given white cowls and white tail bands. In 1944, similar markings appeared on all Allied aircraft. These Invasion markings were to prevent mistaken identity with any German aircraft.

Further refinements to the TYPHOON from the beginning of its service life were relatively few:

1. The bubble canopy was introduced with a sliding hood, resulting in better vision and obviating the 'car-doors' which either used to get stuck or fall open during combat.

2. The de Havilland hydromatic propellor was given four blades instead of three.

3. Successive Sabres delivered gradually more power.

4. The rigid radio mast was replaced by a lowdrag 'whip' aerial behind the canopy instead of coming up out of it.

5. The cannon were more neatly and aerodynamically faired into the wing, and their feed mechanism was made more reliable.

6. Sighting for bombs and rockets was refined.

By D-Day, 6th June, 1944, Gloster had built almost 2,000 TYPHOONS and the 2nd Tactical Air Force had 26 operational TYPHOON Squadrons. The TYPHOON was now coming into its own and justifying the long period of its painful development. With the Allied Invasion of the continent of Europe, the ground forces could call on the services of the TYPHOON in a new form of warfare, cab-rank warfare. By use of radio, ground units could call on R.A.F. TYPHOONS to make their devastating fighter-bomber attacks with bombs, rocket projectiles or cannon on any enemy strong-point, individual tanks or enemy vehicles, that held up their advance.

In the third week of August 1944, TYPHOONS were responsible for smashing practically the whole surviving German army west of the Rhine when the remnants of 16 Divisions (including 9 Panzer Divisions) had been trapped near Falaise, Argentan and Chambois in Northern France. This accounting for the 5th Panzer Army, the 7th Army, and the 'Eberbach' Panzer group. TYPHOONS, mainly from 83 Group (including 174 Squadron along with Peter Watson), simply poured rocket projectiles, cannon and bombs onto the Germans until they were either completely destroyed or totally immobilised. It was the end of Hitler on the western side of the Rhine.

Many TYPHOON Squadrons left their U.K. bases immediately after the D-Day Invasion and encamped just over the Channel in Northern France on hastily prepared airstrips near the coast. These employed steelmesh matting (Sommerfield matting) to enable the aircraft to land and take off.

The August heat caused dust to play havoc with the TYPHOON's sleeve-valve engines, the dust being swirled up into the airducts by the big de Havilland four-bladed propellors. A dynamic ram-type impact filter dome, that kept dust and sand out of the intake-duct to the injection carburettor of the later Sabre II engines, was designed in a mere 12 hours. They went into production the following day. Douglas Dakotas delivered the first batch on the evening of the third day and all TYPHOONS on the Continental airstrips had the new filter fitted by the fifth day. Other TYPHOONS, Peter Watson's included, made the trip back to the U.K. to have new engines fitted.

One of the TYPHOON's unusual engine features was the COFFMAN starter. It was driven by a huge cartridge, there being a magazine of them at the ready for start-ups. An airman would always have to stand by at the ready with a fire-extinguisher in case any fuel leaks were ignited, causing the TYPHOON to catch fire. When the pilot pressed the ignition button, there was a very loud report from the detonation of the Coffman starter-cartridge.

The TYPHOON was also outstanding in its speed of operation. The Sabre engine delivered revs as high as 3,700 or 3,850 rpm, and its peculiar whining sound was unique, giving it a most distinctive sound, a sound that was the death-knell for Hitler's armour in 1944/45.

With the European war won, the TYPHOON disappeared very quickly from the scene, the last, SW 772's, actually being delivered from Gloster, in November 1945. A few were used to tow target banners, others as squadron hacks into 1946 and 1947, and one was used by Napier at Luton for annular radiator trials. But the sole survivor is MN 235, which is proudly on display at the museum at R.A.F. Hendon.

In early 1944, MN 235 had been shipped to Wright Field in the U.S.A. for evaluation by the American Air Force and from there it was passed to the Smithsonian Institute, which returned it to the R.A.F. in 1967 in exchange for a Hawker HURRICANE.

The total production of all TYPHOONS was 3,317.
The name of this famous world war II fighter bomber will live on, for it has been decided that the new Eurofighter will be called the **TYPHOON**.